The Ukule chordlist

C

C#/

D

D#/
Eb

E

F

F#/
Gb

G

G#/
Ab

A

A#/
Bb

B

Fret
Diagram

Moveable
Chords

12-Bar
Blues

© 2011 by Faber Music Ltd
First published by Faber Music Ltd in 2011
Bloomsbury House 74–77 Great Russell Street London WC1B 3DA

Written by Alex Davis

Designed by Lydia Merrills-Ashcroft
Photography by Ben Turner

Printed in England by Caligraving Ltd

ISBN10: 0-571-53605-0
EAN13: 978-0-571-53605-4

To buy Faber Music publications or to find out about the full range
of titles available, please contact your local music retailer or
Faber Music sales enquiries:

Faber Music Ltd, Burnt Mill, Elizabeth Way,
Harlow, CM20 2HX England
Tel: +44(0)1279 82 89 82
Fax: +44(0)1279 82 89 83
sales@fabermusic.com fabermusic.com

History of the Ukulele

Whatever point of view you take, one thing you can't ignore about the Ukulele is that it's fun. It originally comes from Hawaii which is, after all, a pretty fun place. To be even more exact it arrived in Honolulu aboard a ship called the Ravenscrag, carrying 419 Portuguese immigrants from the island of Madeira to work in the sugar cane fields, on the afternoon of August 23, 1879. To alleviate boredom during the long Atlantic sea journey these newcomers had brought with them a few small, four stringed, fretted instruments known as a **Machete de Braga** (sometimes known as a **Machete** or **Braguinha**, a smaller but similar instrument to the modern Cavaquinho) which immediately captured the imagination and hearts of the native Hawaiians – not least of all their King Kalakaua who ended up incorporating Ukulele performances into Royal gatherings! His successor, Queen Lili'uokalani, believed that the word 'Ukulele' meant "the gift that came here" from the Hawaiian words **uku** (gift or reward) and **lele** (to come), although there are many other theories.

Three of the newcomers had been cabinet makers back in Maderira and had no difficulty in transferring their skills to Ukulele manufacture by the mid-1880s. Things must have gone crazy from that point – by the time Hawaii had joined the United States in 1900 the Ukulele was by far and away the island's most popular instrument. The Hawaiian exhibit at the Panama-Pacific International Exposition of 1915 did much to open American eyes to this island of sunshine and Ukuleles, and it didn't take long for Hollywood studios and Tin Pan Alley songwriters to start using the instrument in films and songs. Stars such as Cliff Edwards in the US and George Formby in the UK helped popularise the Ukulele beyond even the guitar, (sheet music from the '20s and '30s generally features Uke chords!), and mainstream instrument manufacturers such as Martin and Gibson were knocking out thousands of them.

The Ukulele has had its ups and downs since then – the Great Depression saw a fall in popularity, followed by renewed interest after the 2nd World War, helped by Maccaferri's manufacture of cheap plastic Ukes, television performances by Arthur Godfrey and the memorable recordings of Tiny Tim. Things tailed off again by the end of the '60s – rock'n'roll had placed the guitar at the forefront of the popular musician's arsenal and the social/political unrest surrounding things like the Vietnam war didn't really go hand-in-hand with the cheerful sound of the Uke. Things changed yet again in the '90s with all kinds of musicians around the world bringing the instrument back into the public eye (ranging from traditional Hawaiian artists like Israel Kamakawiwo'ole to the Ukulele Orchestra Of Great Britain, not to mention a good few Indie bands), many new manufacturers bringing out Ukes at prices to suit everyone, and the likes of George Harrison and Paul McCartney singing the praises of the Ukulele to us all.

Tuning

The standard Ukulele string tuning is G–C–E–A, shown here on the treble stave and piano keyboard. Note that the G string is tuned higher than the C string.

You can tune your Ukulele using a piano or keyboard (or any other instrument that you know is in tune!) or by using an electronic chromatic tuner.

If just one string on your Ukulele is in tune then you can use it to tune the other strings as well.

This diagram shows which fretted notes match the note of the open string above. Eg. Pluck the first string at the 5th fret and match the note to the second open string, and so on.

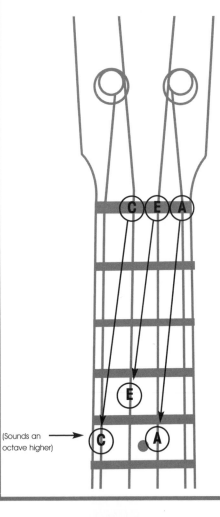

(Sounds an octave higher)

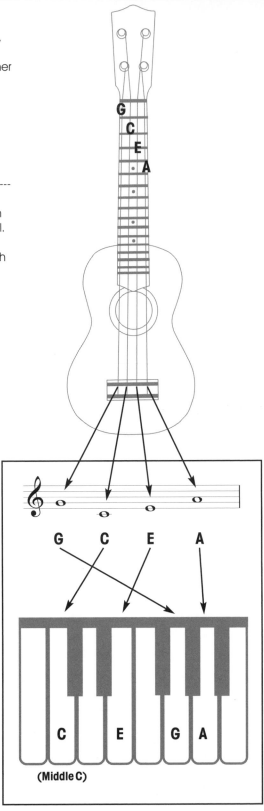

(Middle C)

Reading Chord Boxes

A chord box is basically a diagram of how a chord is played on the neck of the Ukulele. It shows you which string to play, where to put your fingers and whereabouts on the neck the chord is played.

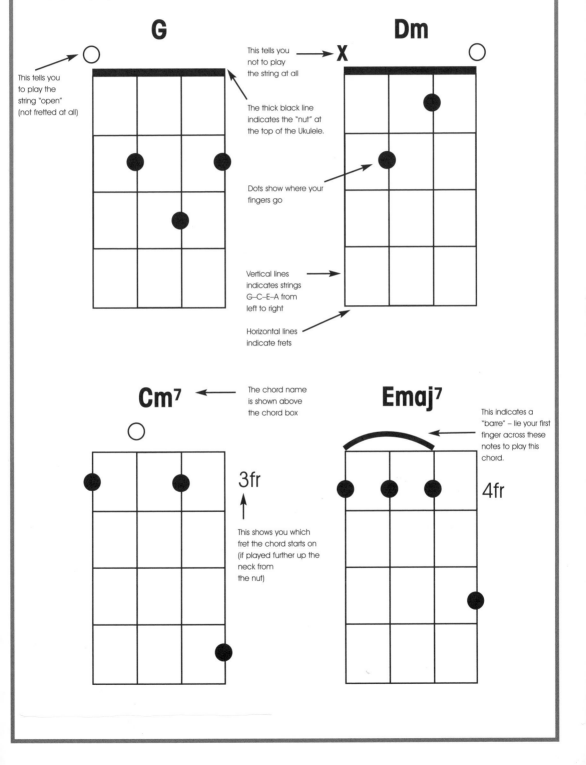

C chords

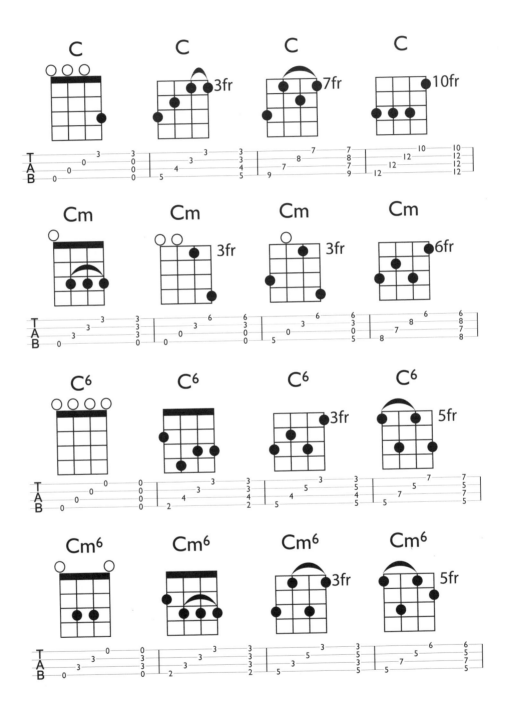

C chords

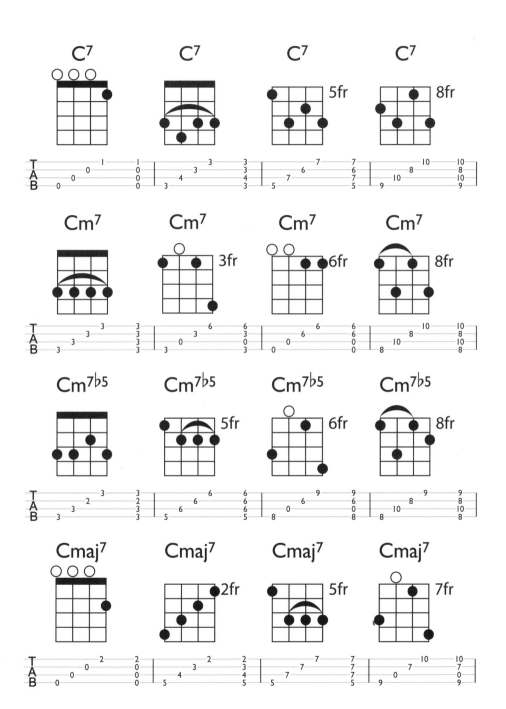

7

C chords

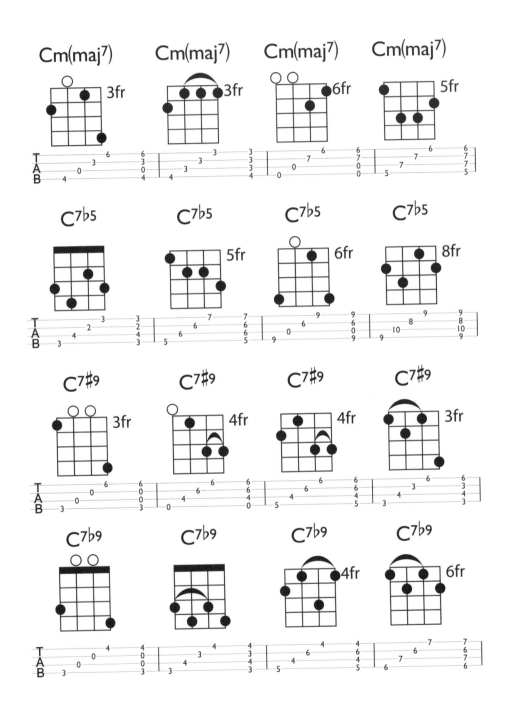

C chords

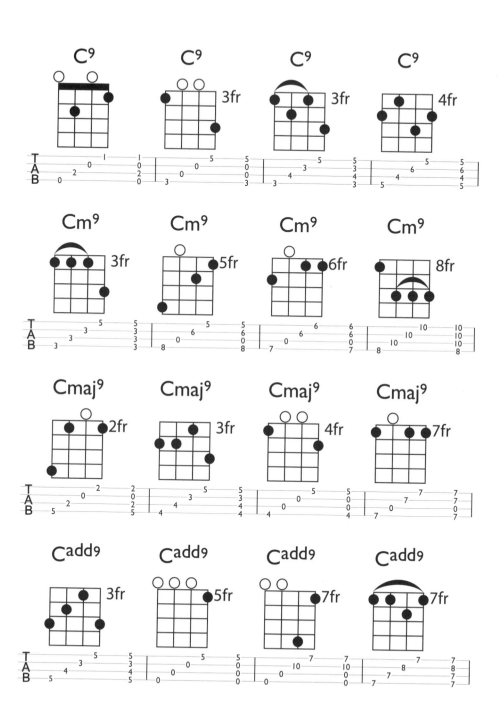

C chords

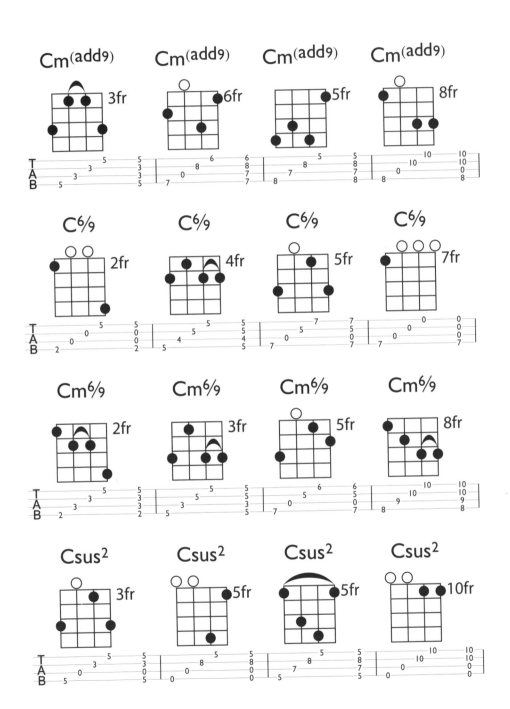

C chords

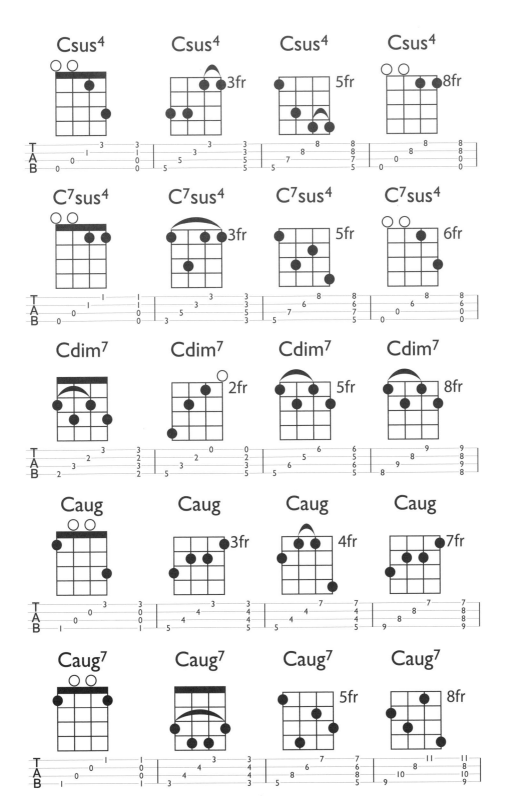

C#/Db chords

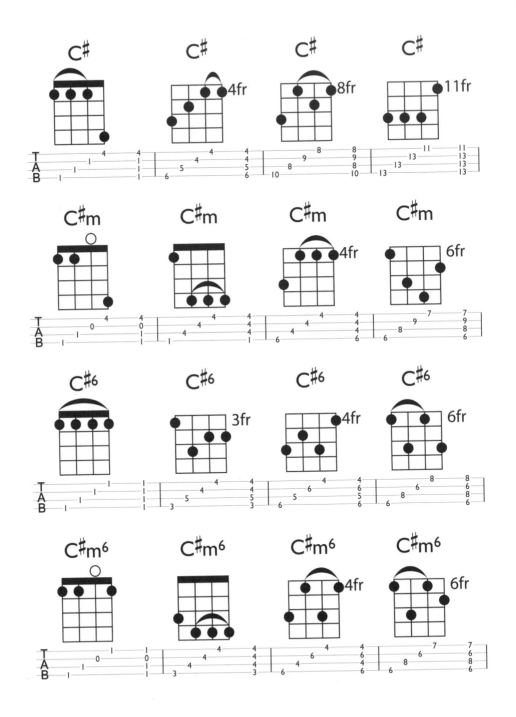

C♯/D♭ chords

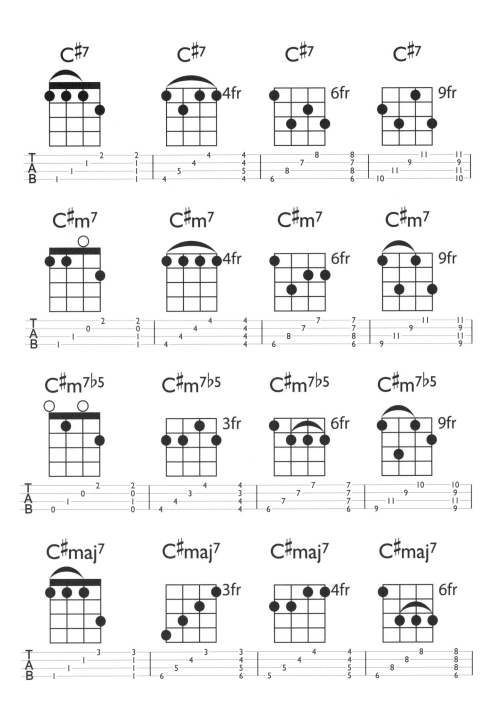

C♯/D♭ chords

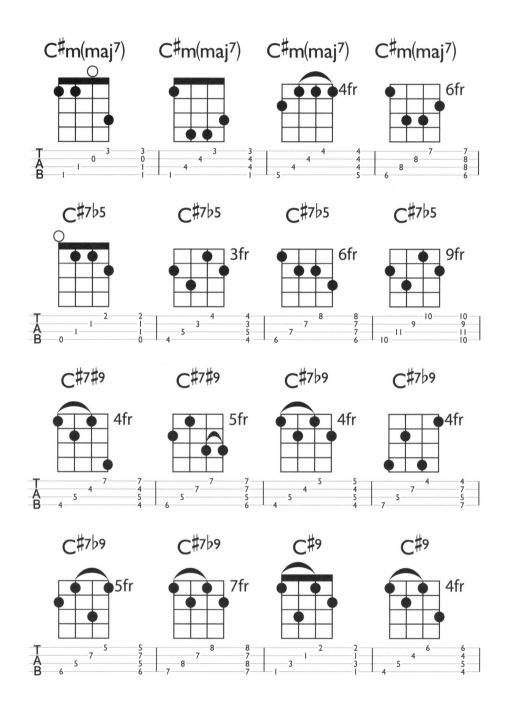

C#/Db chords

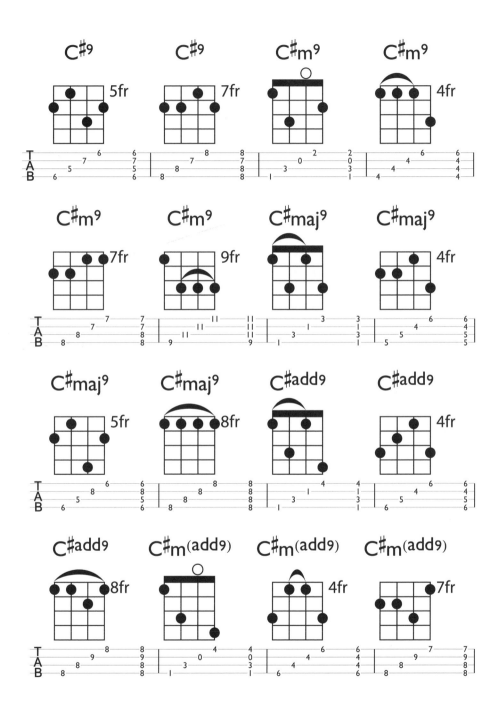

C#/Db chords

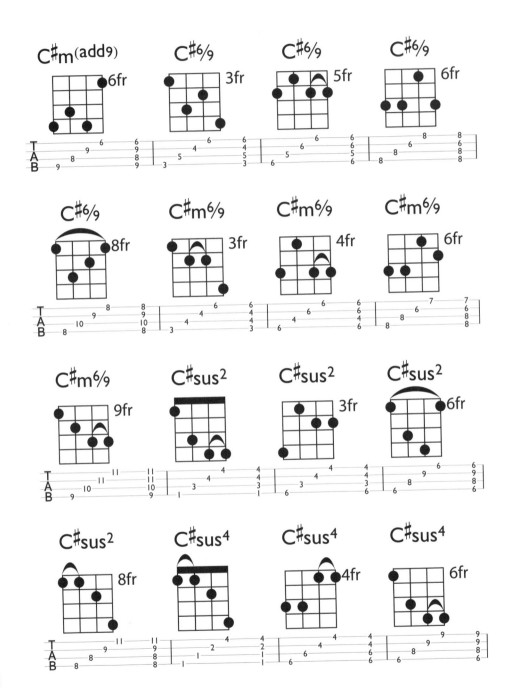

C♯/D♭ chords

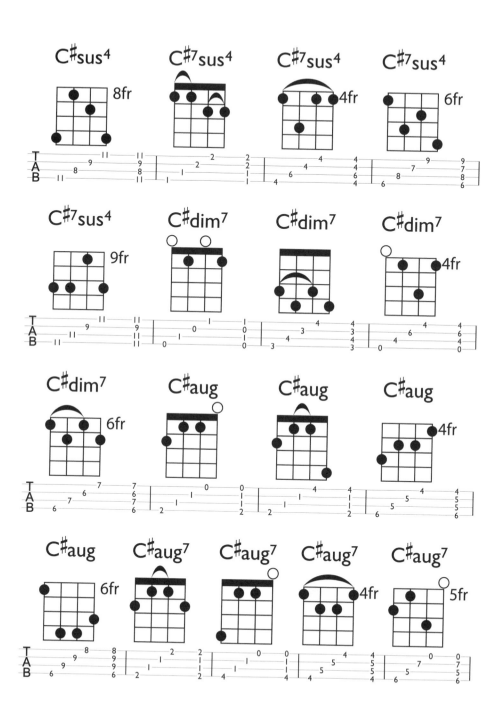

D chords

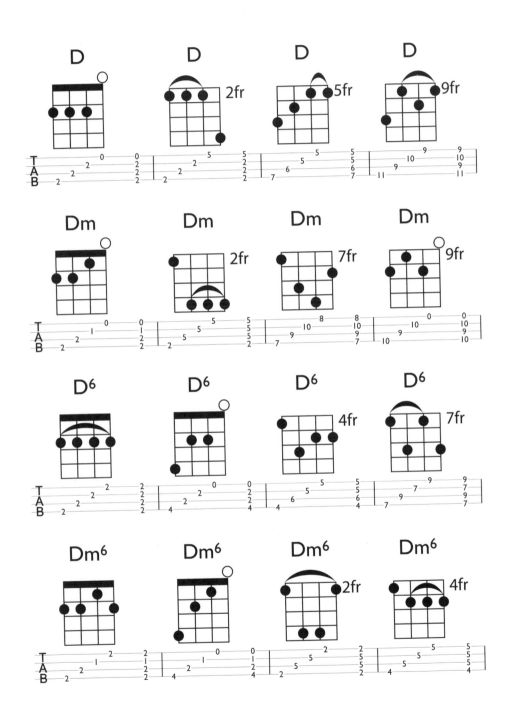

D chords

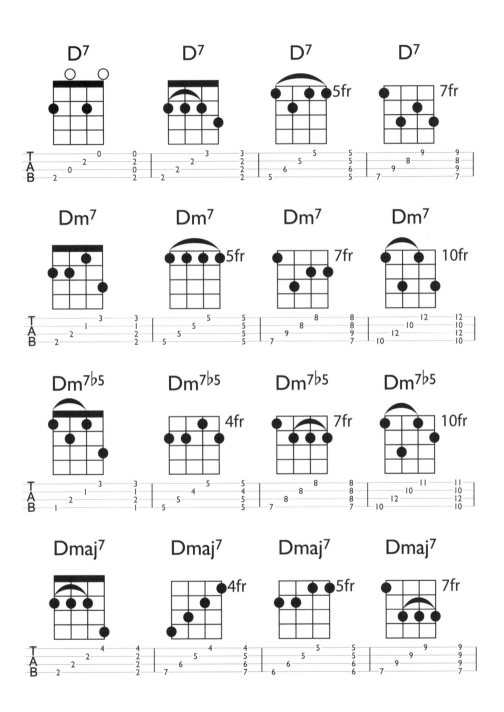

D chords

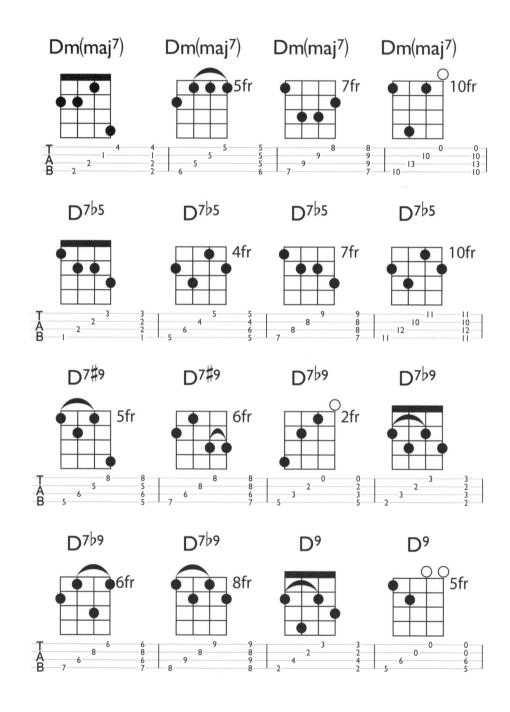

D chords

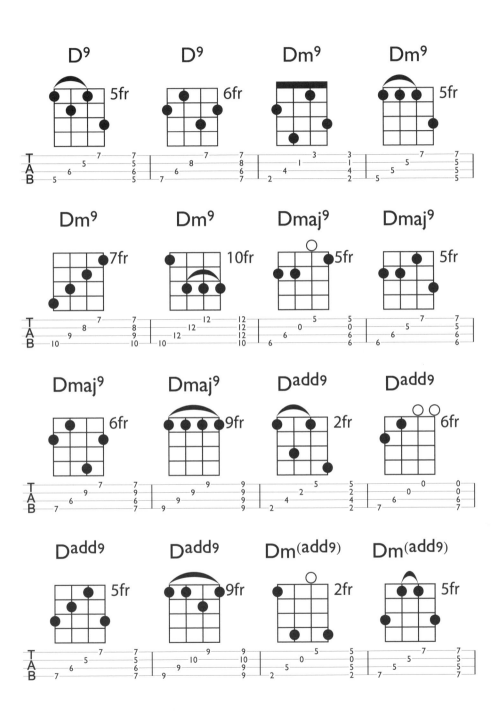

D chords

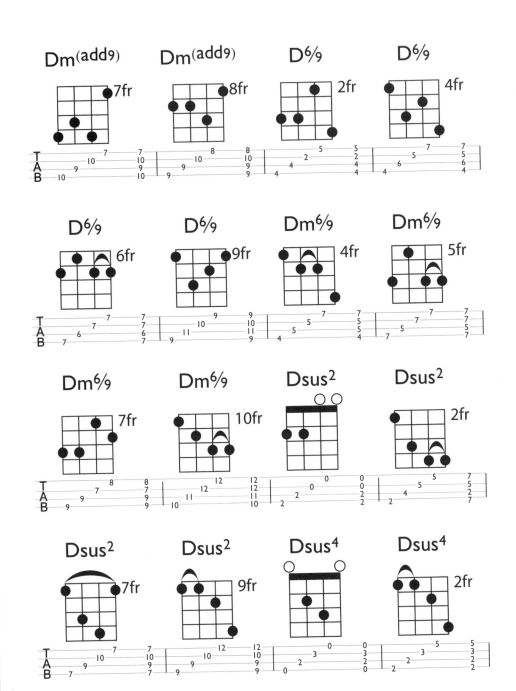

D chords

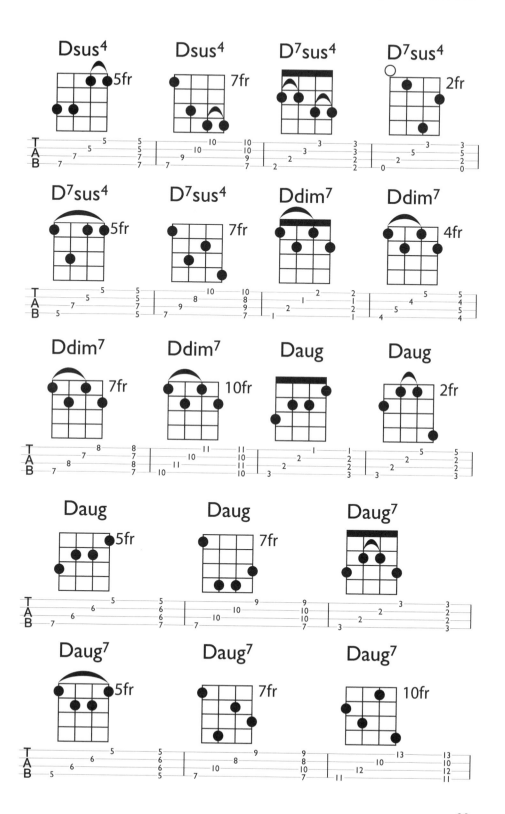

D♯/E♭ chords

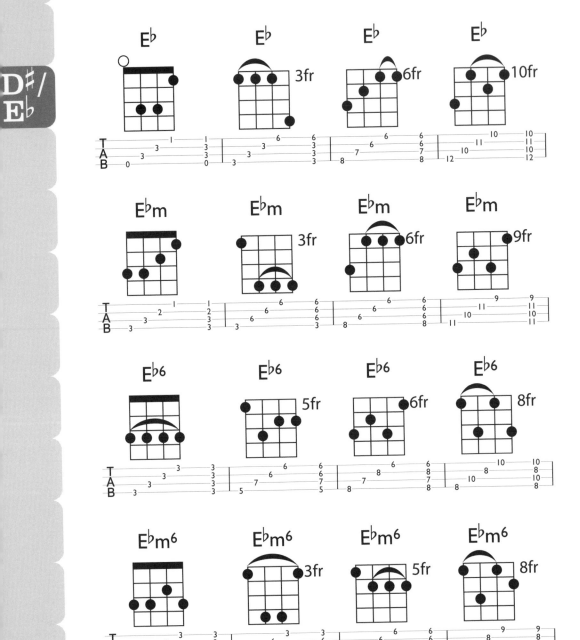

D♯/E♭ chords

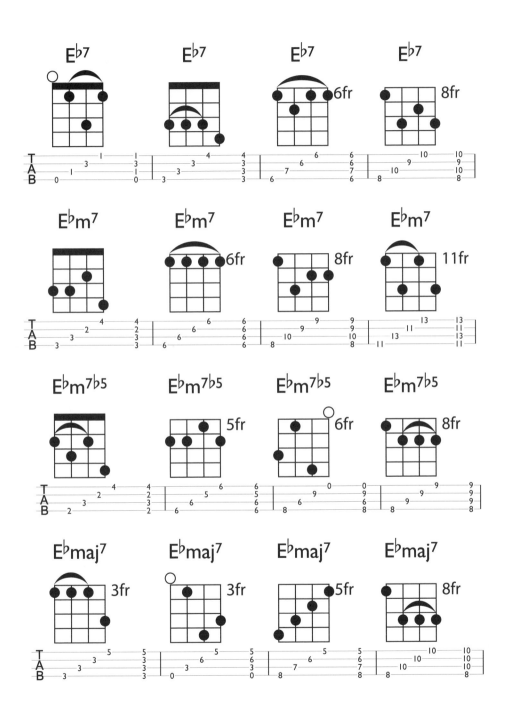

25

D#/E♭ chords

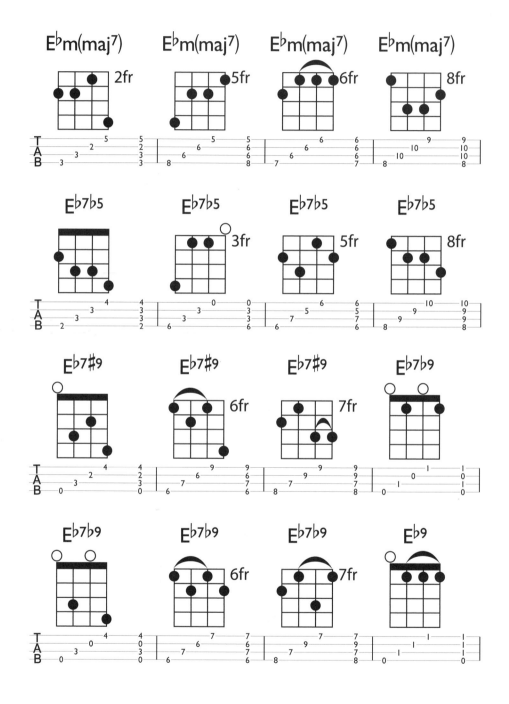

E♭m(maj7)   E♭m(maj7)   E♭m(maj7)   E♭m(maj7)

E♭7♭5   E♭7♭5   E♭7♭5   E♭7♭5

E♭7♯9   E♭7♯9   E♭7♯9   E♭7♭9

E♭7♭9   E♭7♭9   E♭7♭9   E♭9

D♯/E♭ chords

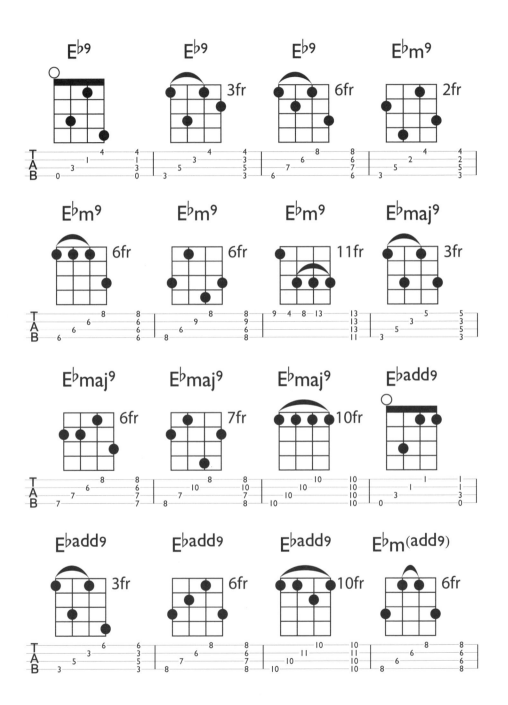

D#/E♭ chords

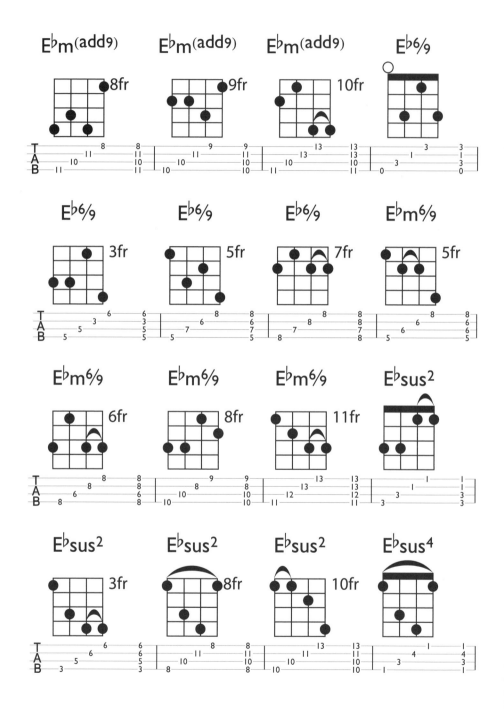

28

D♯/E♭ chords

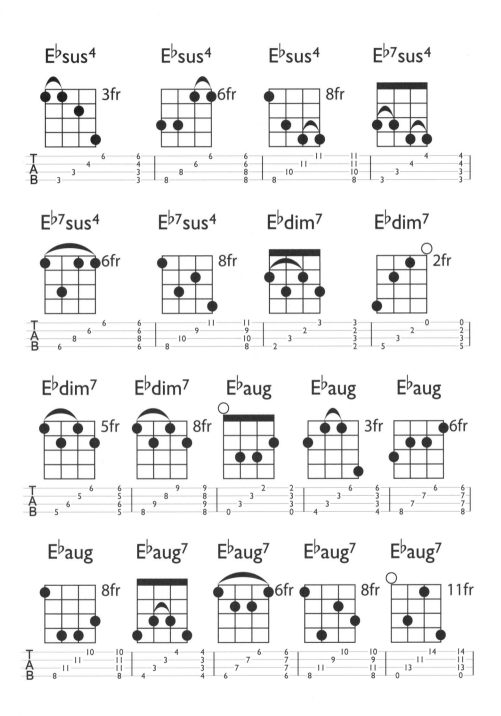

E chords

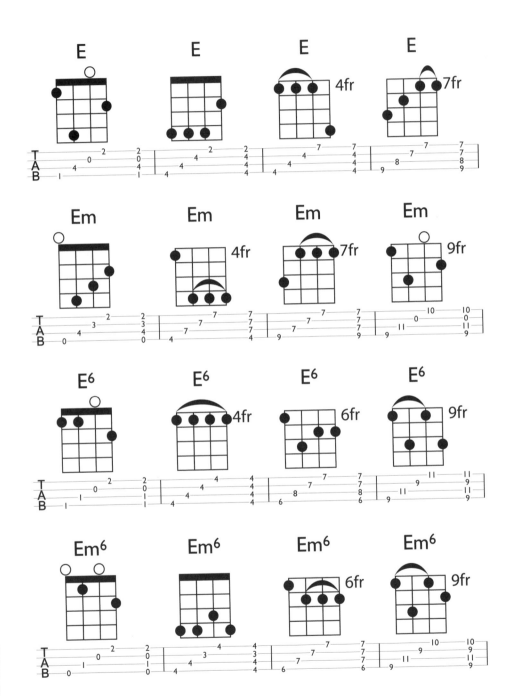

E chords

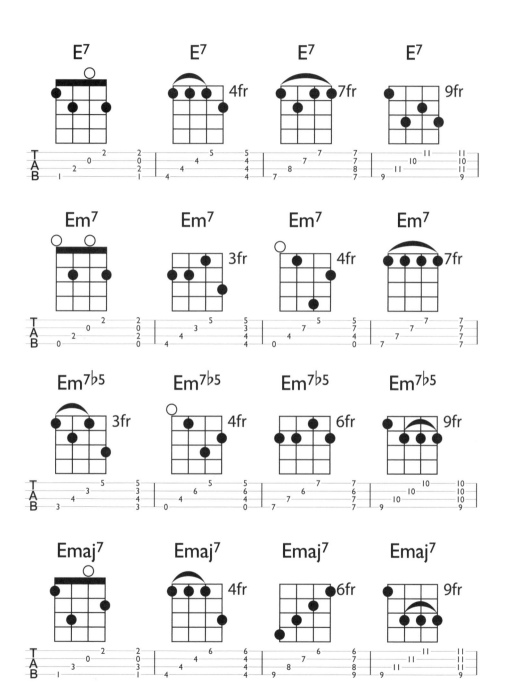

E chords

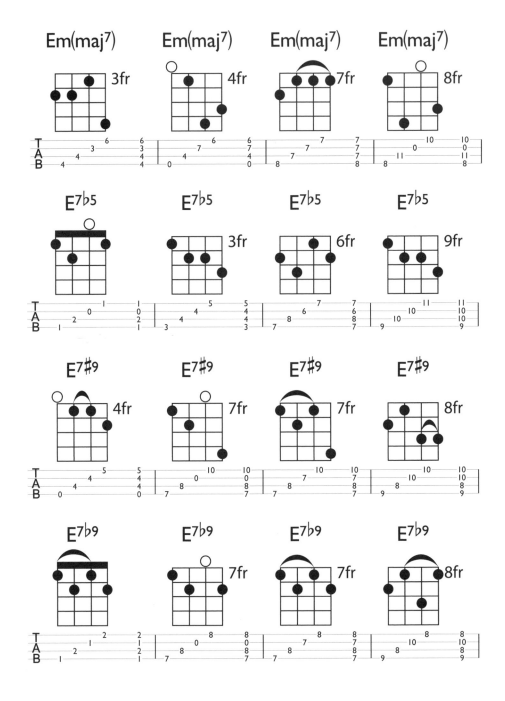

E chords

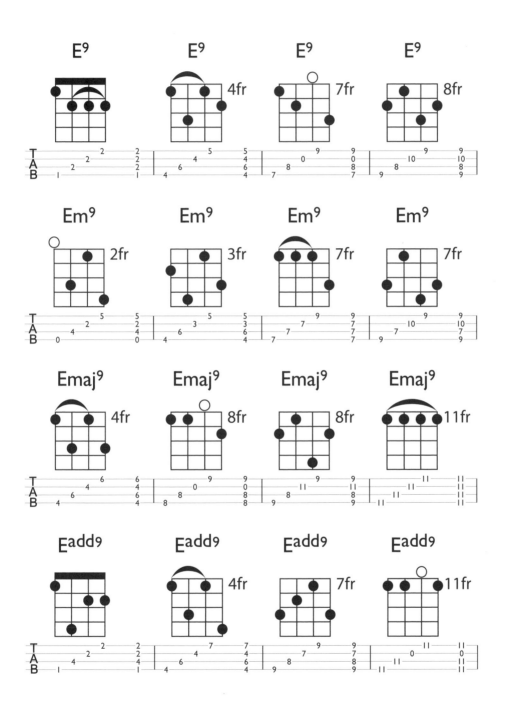

E chords

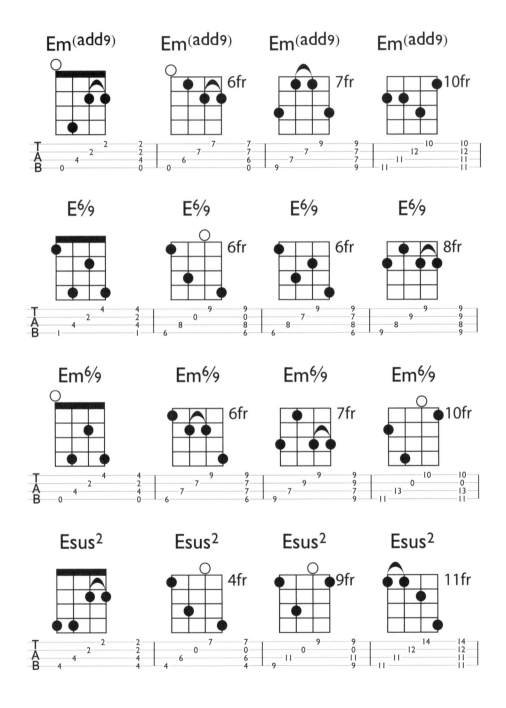

E chords

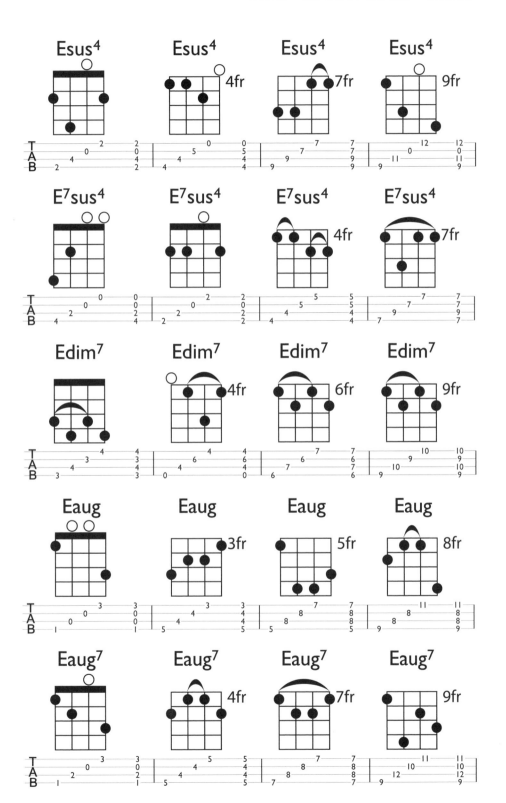

F chords

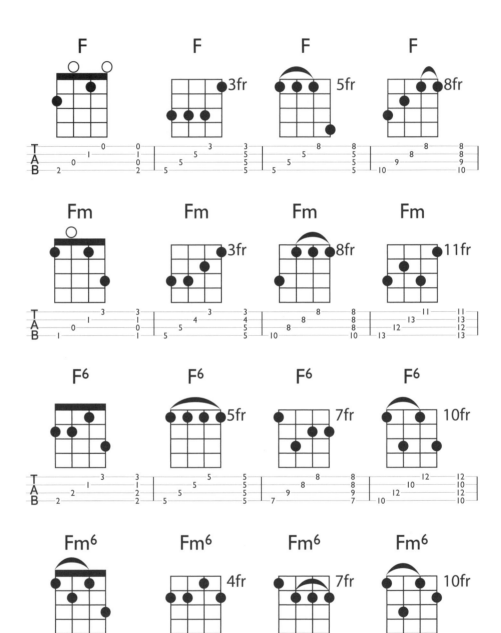

F chords

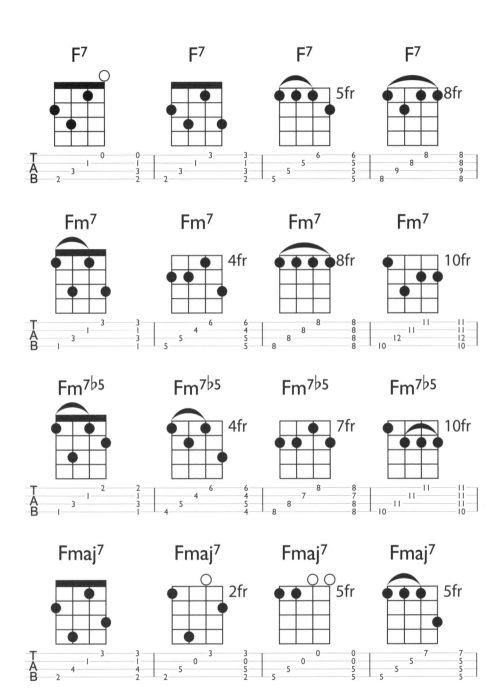

F chords

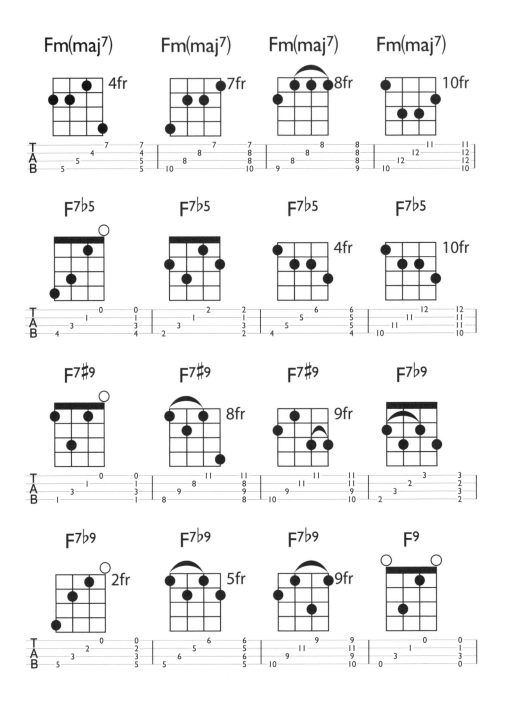

F chords

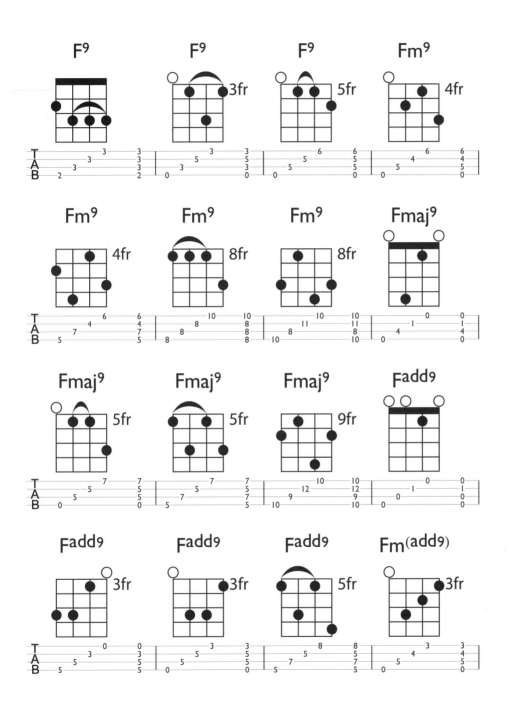

F chords

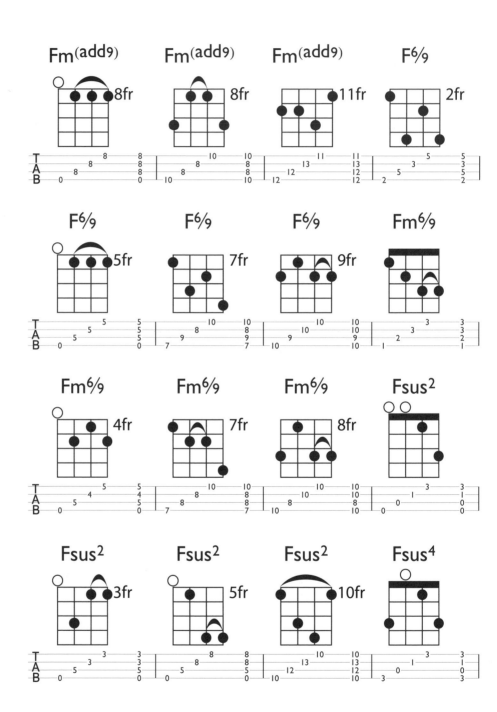

F chords

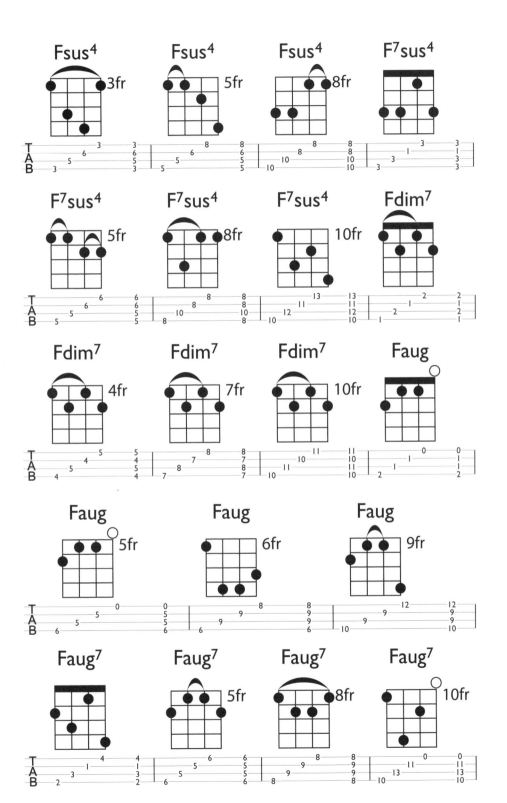

F♯/G♭ chords

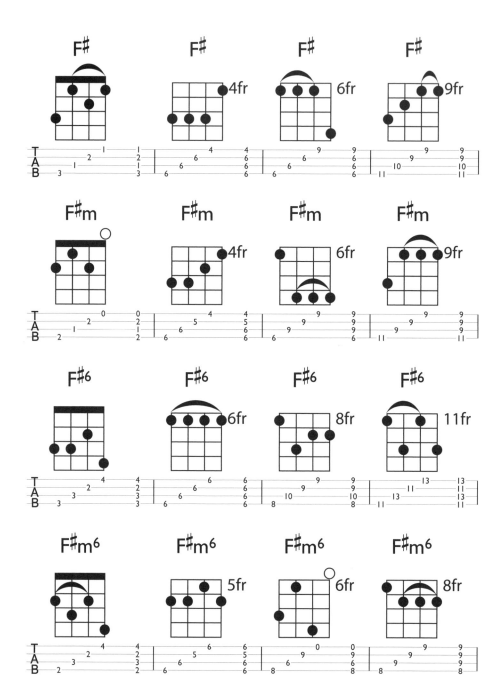

F#/Gb chords

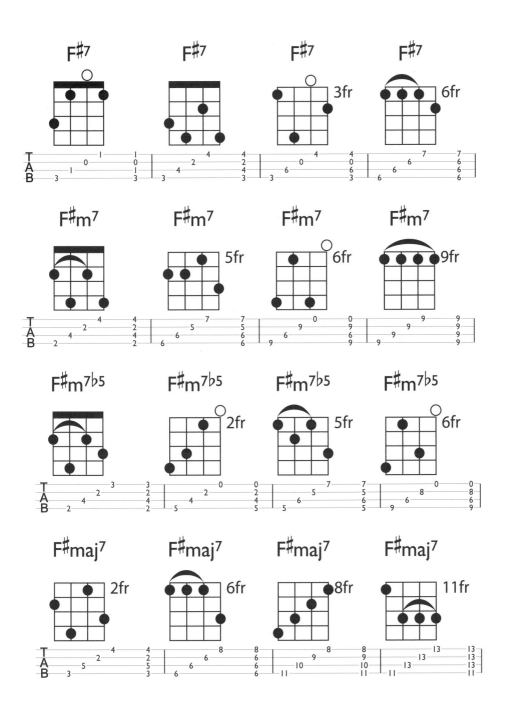

F#/G♭ chords

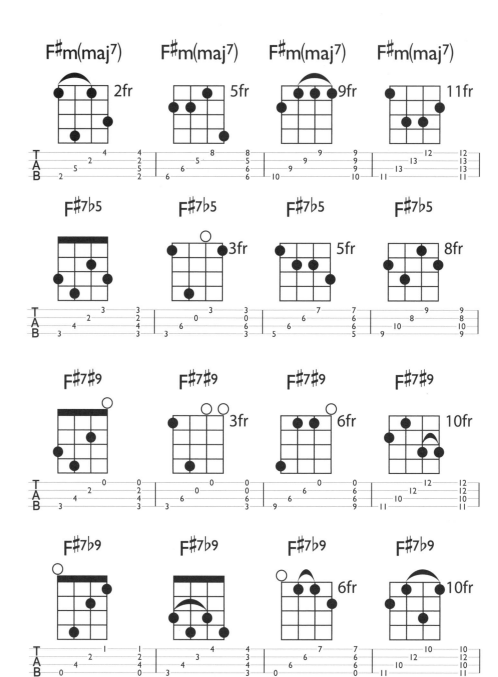

F#/G♭ chords

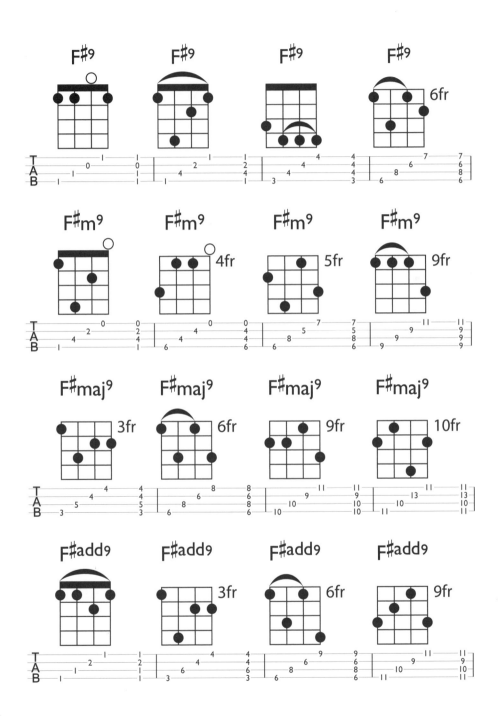

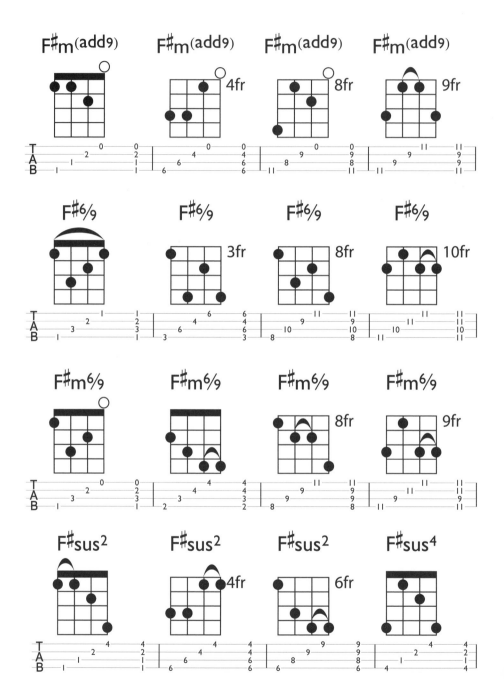

F#m(add9) F#m(add9) F#m(add9) F#m(add9)

F#6/9 F#6/9 F#6/9 F#6/9

F#m6/9 F#m6/9 F#m6/9 F#m6/9

F#sus2 F#sus2 F#sus2 F#sus4

F#/Gb

F♯/G♭ chords

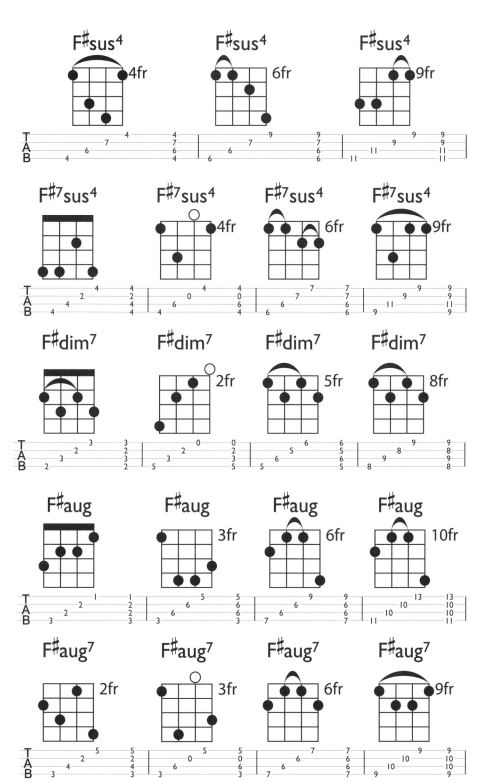

G chords

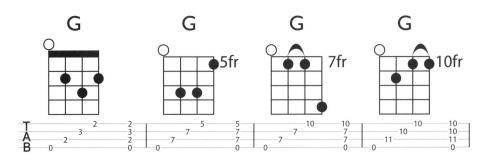

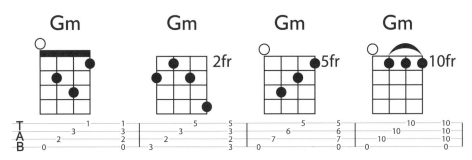

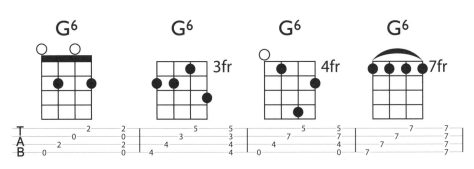

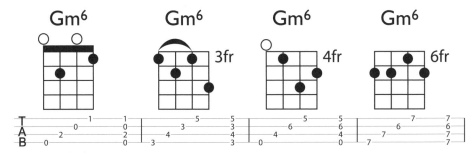

G

48

G chords

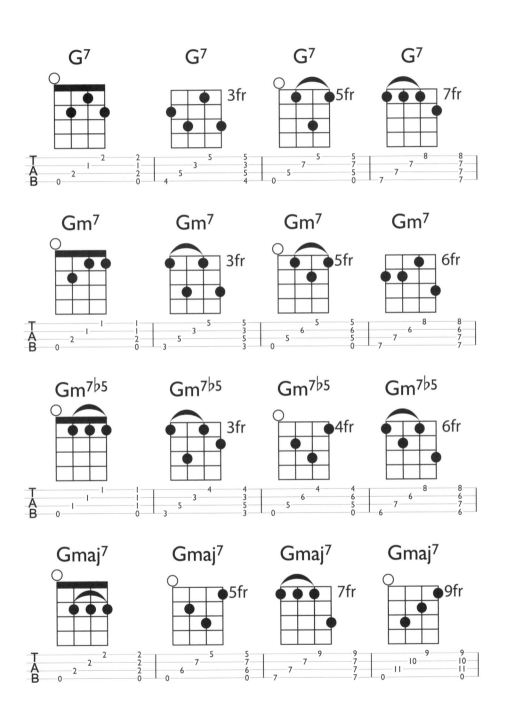

G chords

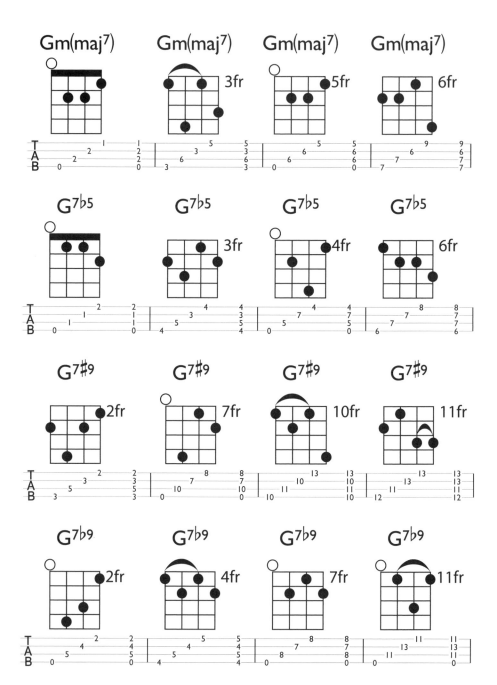

G chords

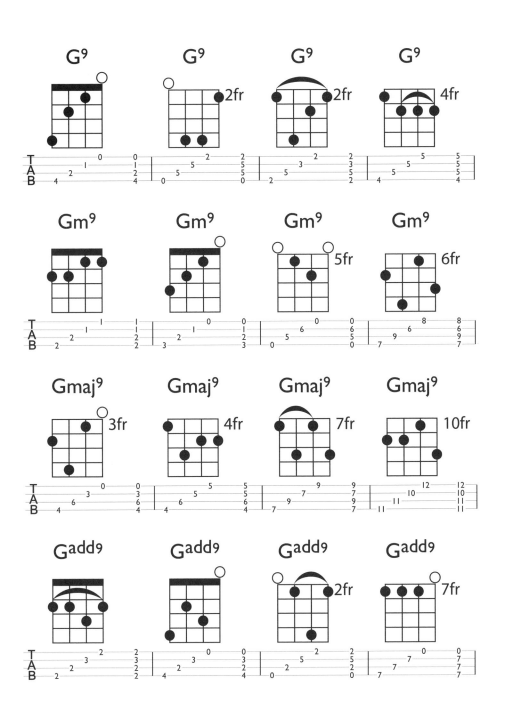

G chords

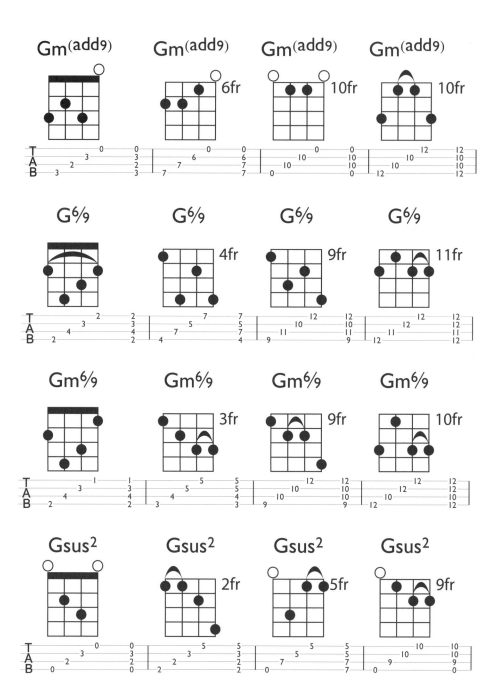

G chords

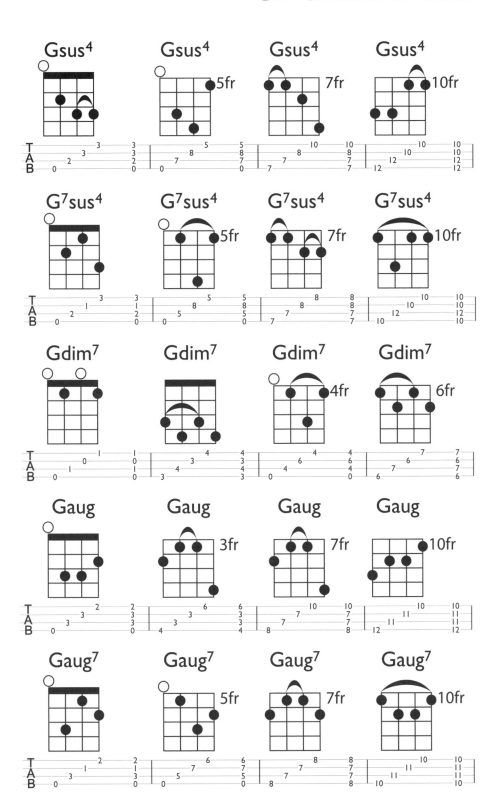

G♯/A♭ chords

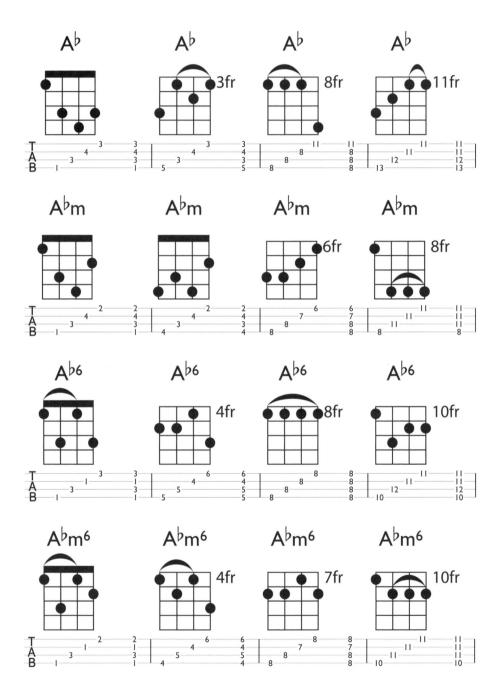

G$^\sharp$/A$^\flat$ chords

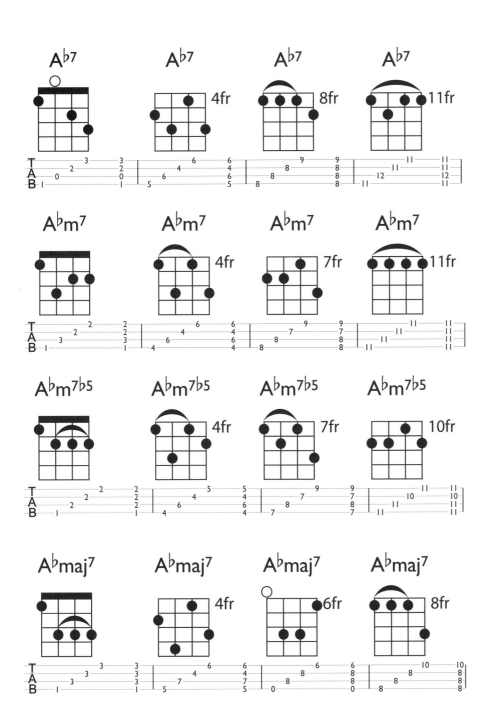

G♯/A♭ chords

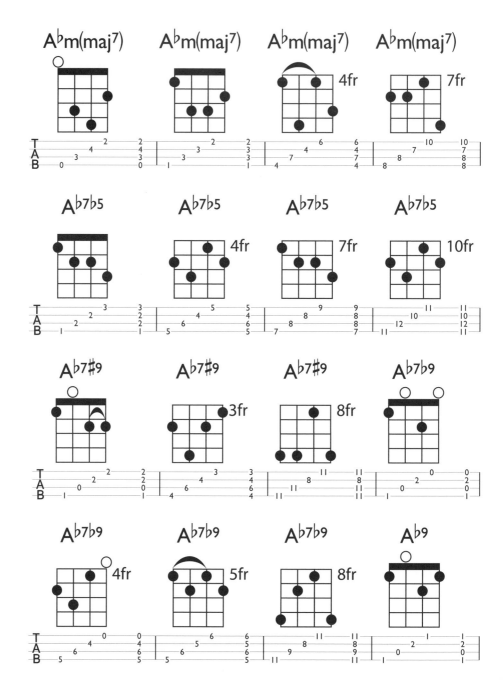

G♯/A♭ chords

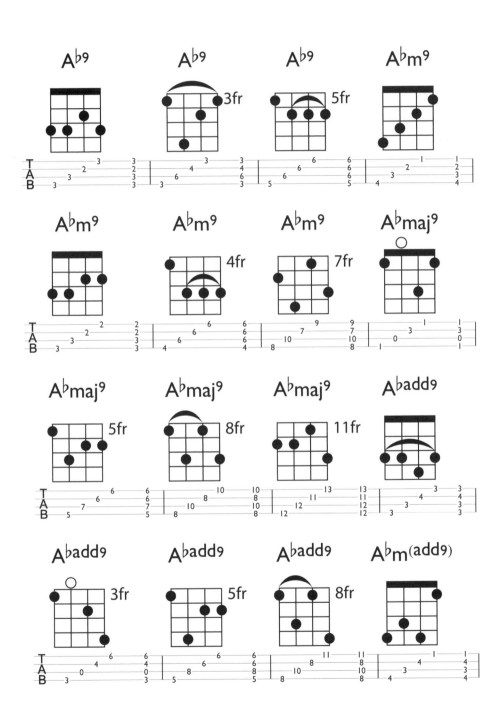

G#/A♭ chords

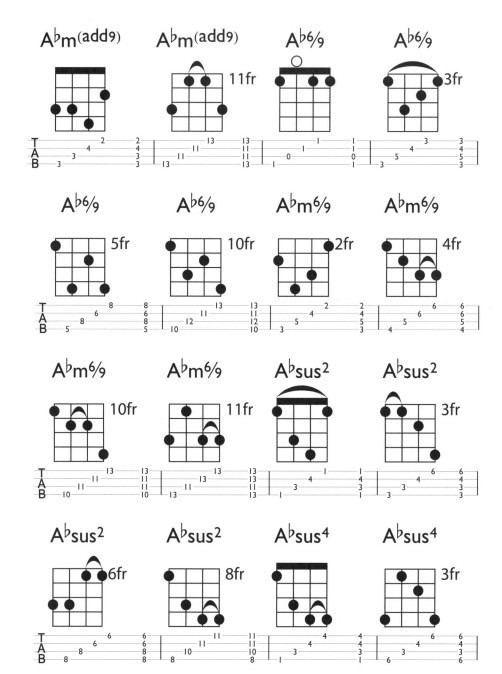

G♯/A♭ chords

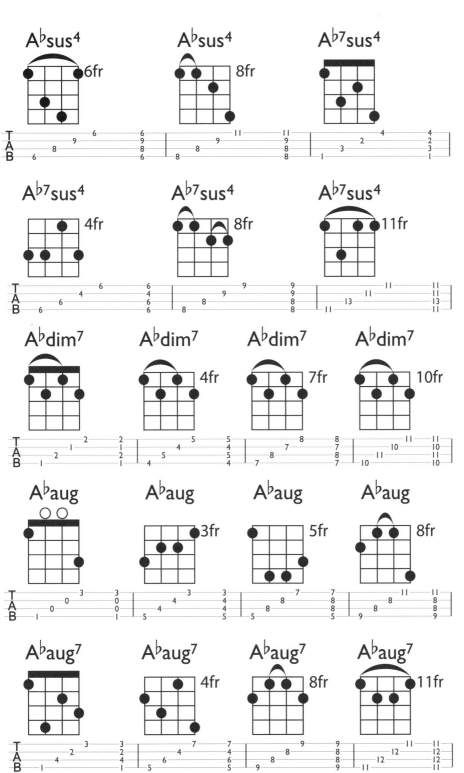

A chords

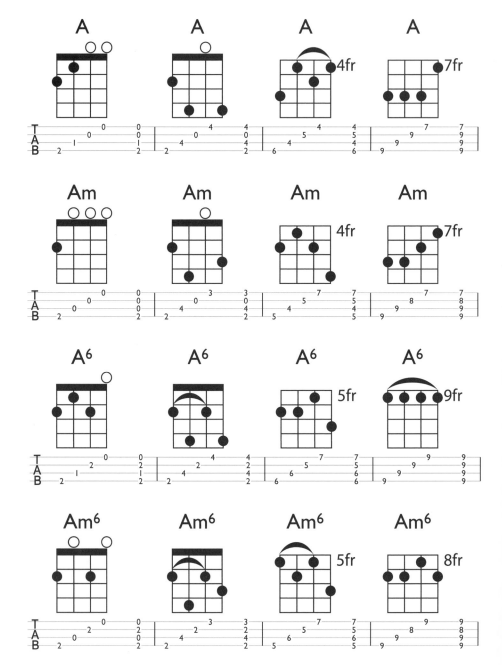

A chords

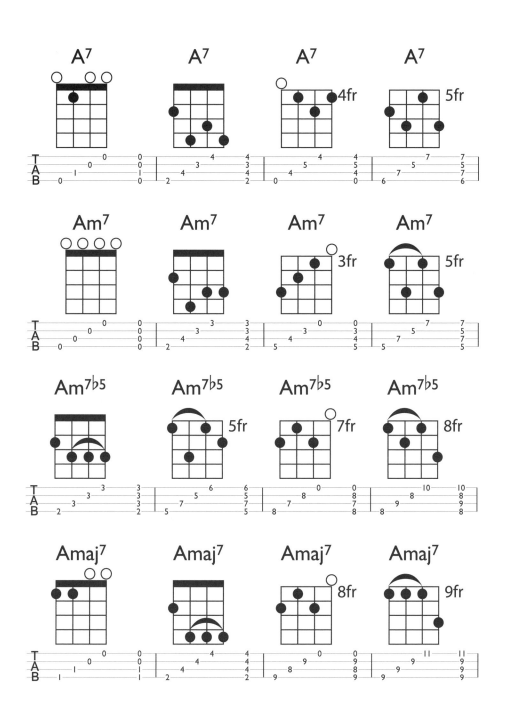

A chords

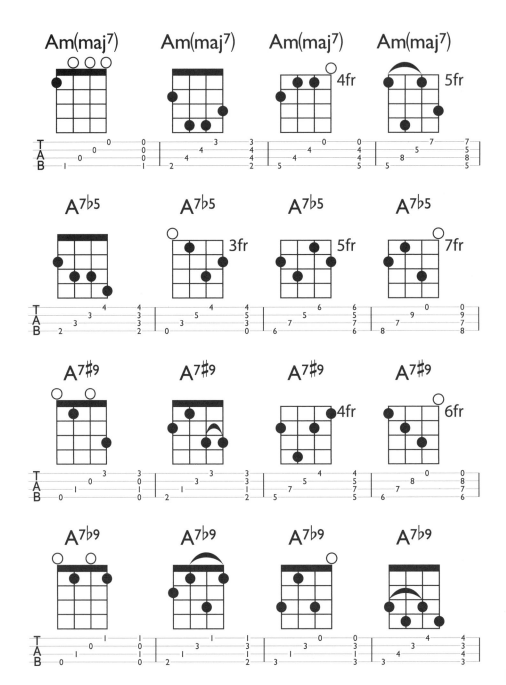

A chords

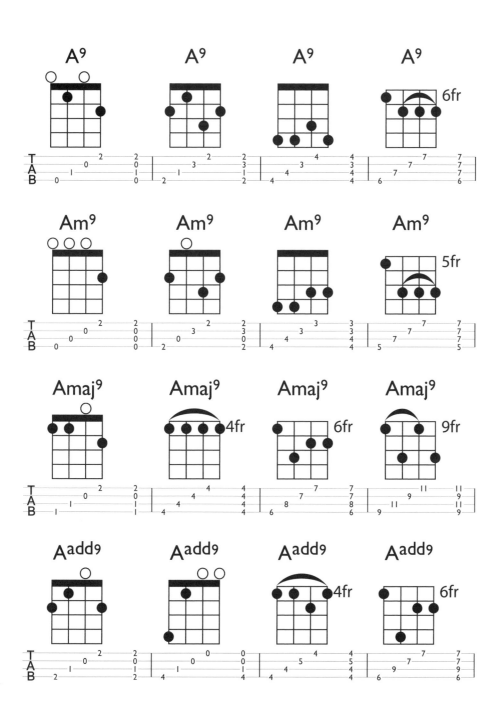

A chords

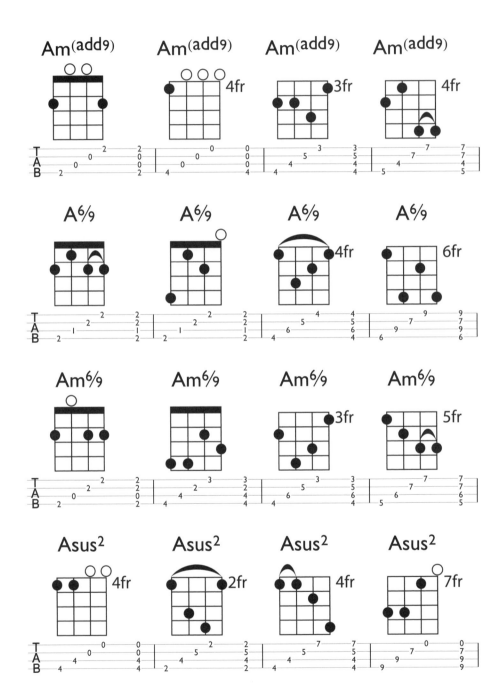

A chords

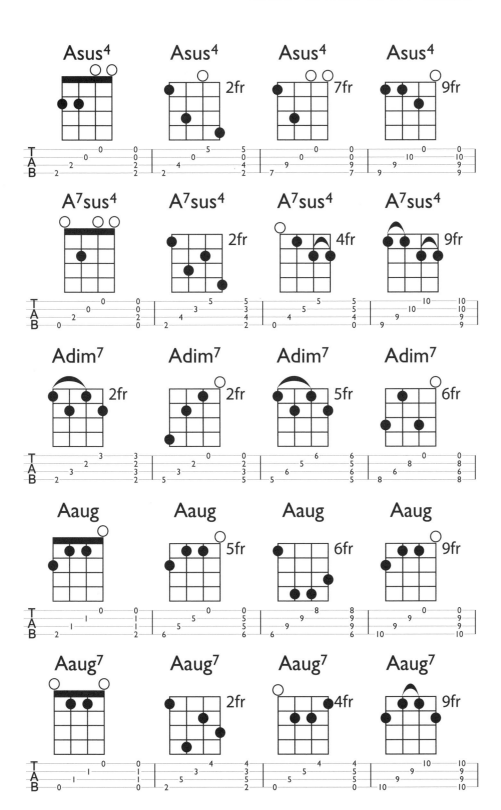

A#/B♭ chords

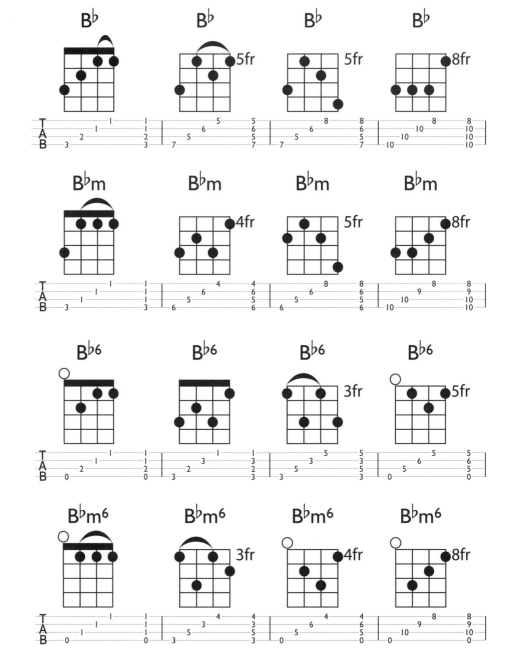

A♯/B♭ chords

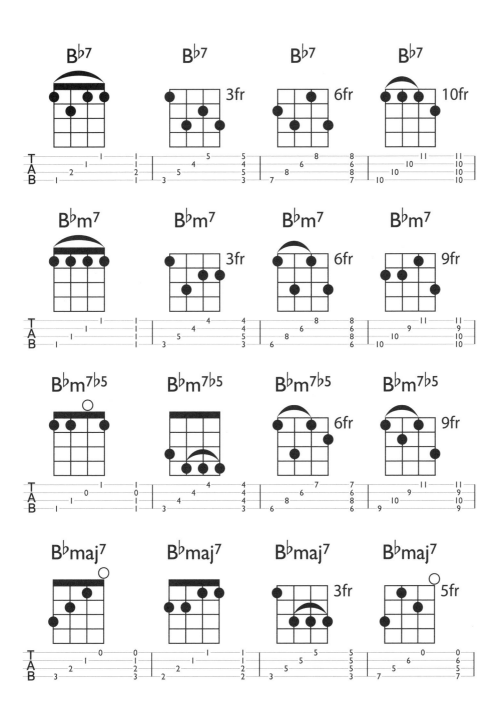

A♯/B♭ chords

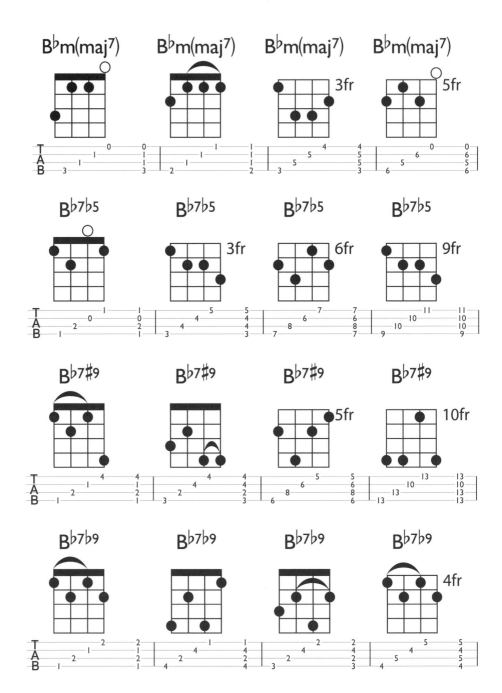

A♯/B♭ chords

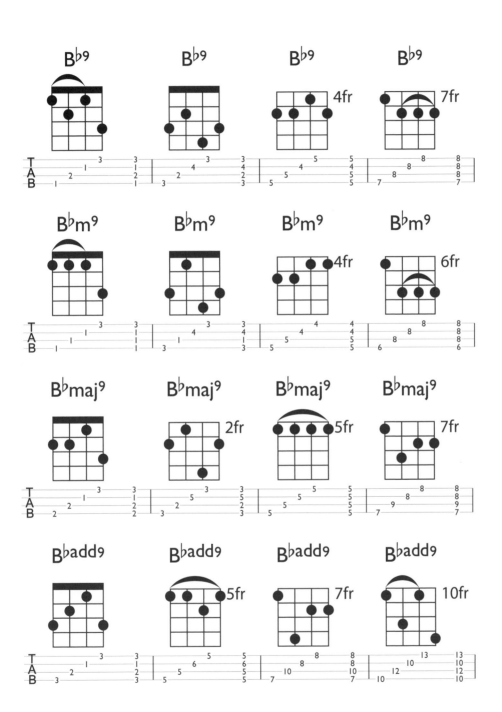

A♯/B♭ chords

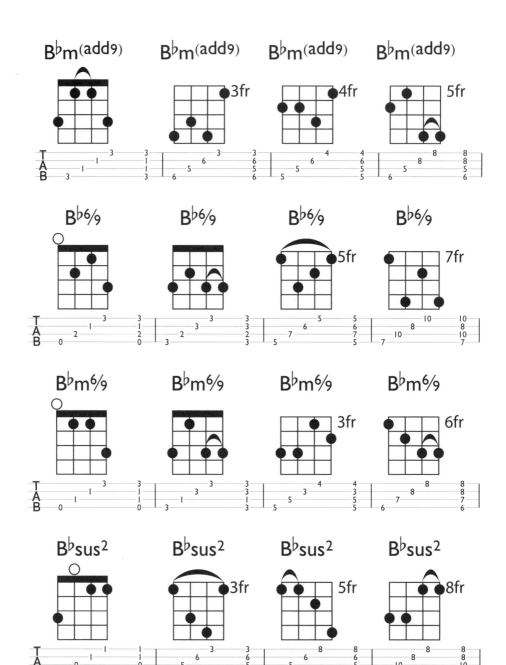

A♯/B♭ chords

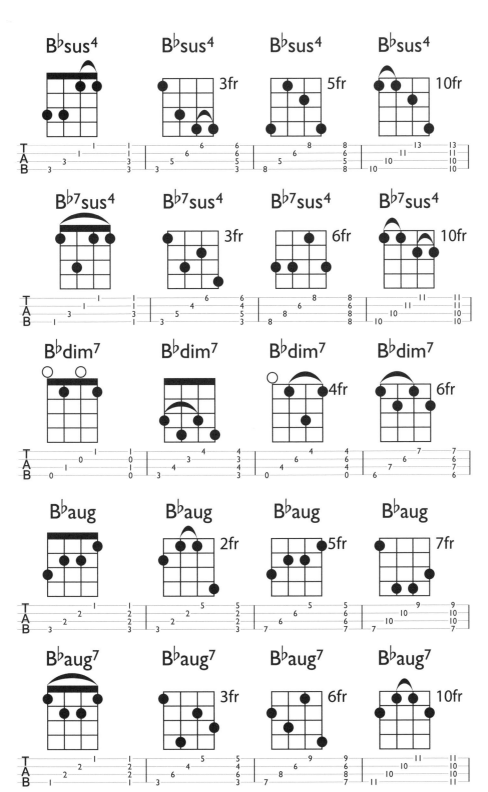

B chords

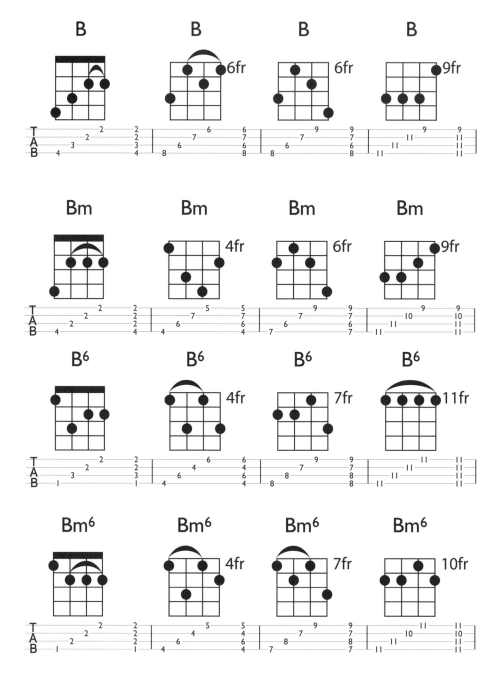

B chords

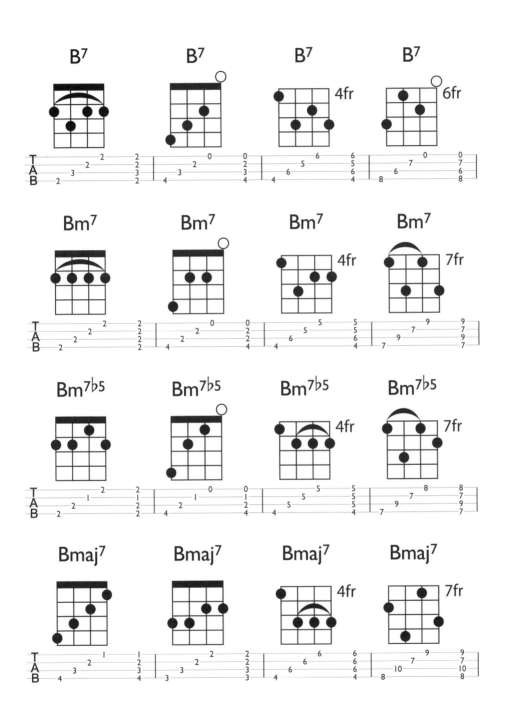

B chords

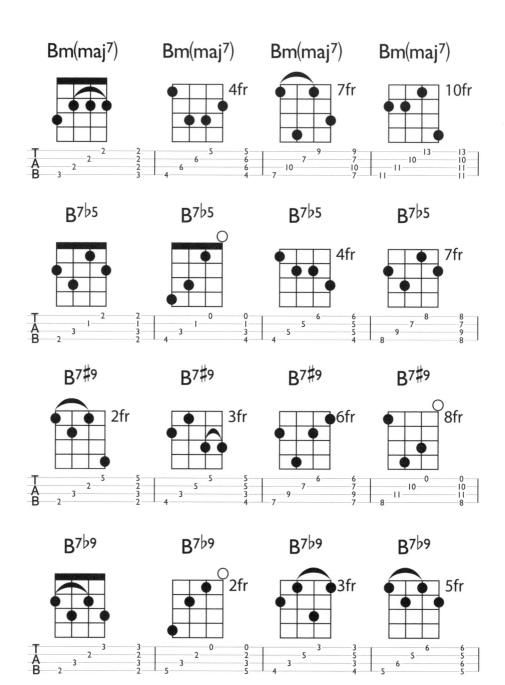

B chords

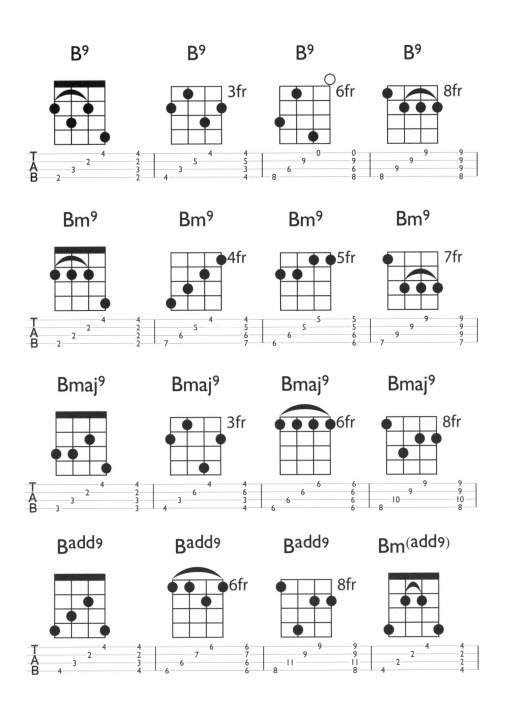

B chords

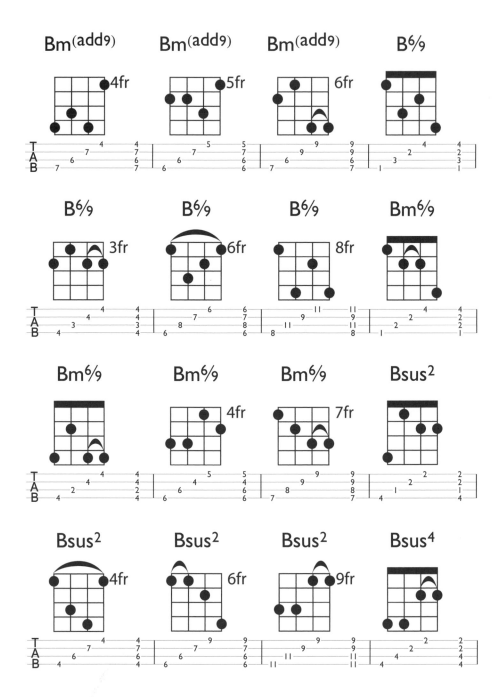

B chords

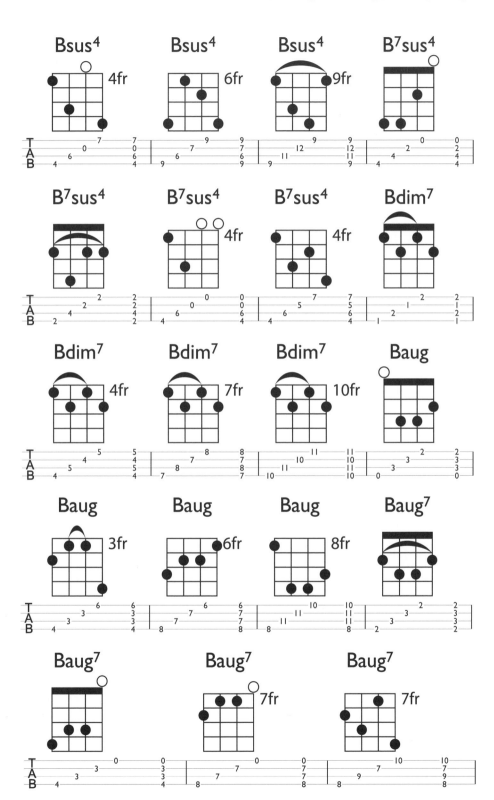

Moveable Chords & 12-Bar Blues

Fret
Diagram

Moveable
Chords

12-Bar
Blues

Chord shapes that use all four strings of the Ukulele can be regarded as 'moveable' chords, i.e. you can move the same shape up and down the neck of your Uke to produce different chords. We've listed many useful moveable chord shapes for you (see pages 81–85), many of which you'll probably recognise from the main part of this book.

This diagram of your Ukulele fretboard shows you the position of every note on the neck up to the 13th fret. All the moveable chords have got the the main or 'root' note indicated (some even have 2 root notes – high and low) – simply match the root note to whatever key you want your chord to sound in.

Some chord shapes appear more than once in this collection (e.g. three of the 6th and minor 7th chords) – this is because the same shape can, in some circumstances, be used for different chords with a different root note.

g	C	E	A
G#/Ab	C#/Db	F	A#/Bb
A	D	F#/Gb	B
A#/Bb	D#/Eb	G	C
B	E	G#/Ab	C#/Db
C	F	A	D
C#/Db	F#/Gb	A#/Bb	D#/Eb
D	G	B	E
D#/Eb	G#/Ab	C	F
E	A	C#/Db	F#/Gb
F	A#/Bb	D	G
F#/Gb	B	D#/Eb	G#/Ab
G	C	E	A
G#/Ab	C#/Db	F	A#/Bb

Moveable Chords

Major

Minor

6th

Minor 6th

7th

Moveable Chords

Minor 7th

Minor 7(♭5)

Major 7th

Minor (maj7)

7(♭5)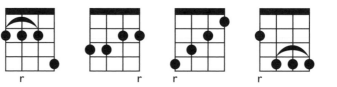

Moveable Chords

7 (#9)

7 (b9)

9th

Minor 9th

Major 9th

Moveable Chords

Major add⁹

r

r

r

r

Minor add⁹

r

r

r

Major add⁶/⁹

r

r
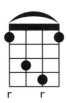
r

Minor add⁶/⁹

r

r

sus²

r

r

r   r

r

Moveable Chords

sus⁴

7 sus⁴

Dim 7th

Aug

Aug 7th

12-Bar Blues

The 12-bar blues is one of the most popular chord progressions in popular music, providing the structure for literally thousands of famous songs, including 'Folsom Prison Blues' by Johnny Cash and 'Johnny B Goode' by Chuck Berry. It can be played in any key using only three chords – the root, the 4th and the 5th – so in the key of C this would be C major, F major and G major.

Cmaj 12-Bar Blues

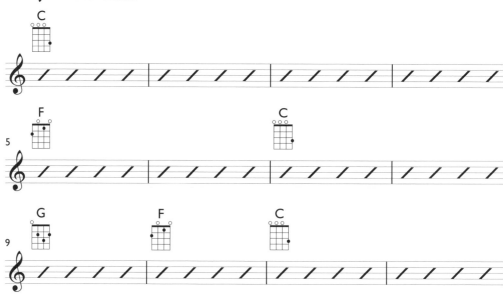

It's easy to play a 12-bar blues in any key – you can work out what the root, 4th and 5th chords are from any fret position by using the neck of your Ukulele and this diagram below. The diagram shows how to find the notes on which to base your root, 4th & 5th chords, in relation to the position of the root note. See also the fretboard diagram on page 80.

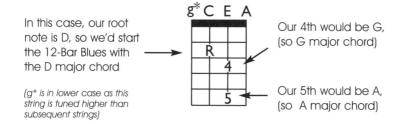

In this case, our root note is D, so we'd start the 12-Bar Blues with the D major chord

(g* is in lower case as this string is tuned higher than subsequent strings)

Our 4th would be G, (so G major chord)

Our 5th would be A, (so A major chord)

The position of the 4th and 5th chords in relation to the root remains the same, right up and down the fingerboard.

12-Bar Blues

Gmaj 12-Bar Blues

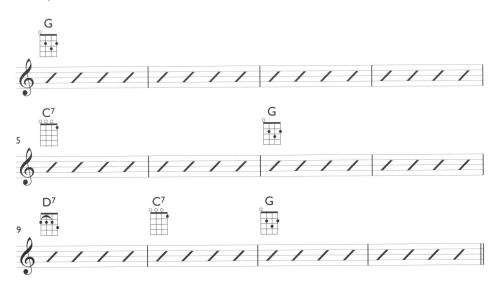

A⁷ 12-Bar Blues

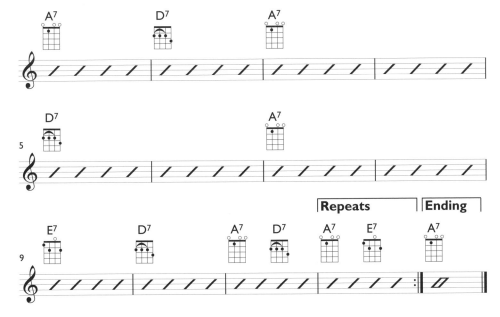